W9-ABG-633

Elections

Locating the Author's Main Idea

Curriculum Consultant: JoAnne Buggey, Ph.D.
College of Education, University of Minnesota

By Neal Bernards

Greenhaven Press, Inc.
Post Office Box 289009
San Diego, CA 92198-9009

Titles in the opposing viewpoints juniors series:

Advertising	The Environment	Population
AIDS	Forests	Poverty
Alcohol	Free Speech	Prisons
Animal Rights	Garbage	Smoking
Causes of Crime	Gun Control	Television
Child Abuse	The Homeless	Toxic Wastes
Christopher Columbus	Immigration	The U.S. Constitution
Death Penalty	Nuclear Power	The War on Drugs
Drugs and Sports	The Palestinian Conflict	Working Mothers
Elections	Patriotism	Zoos
Endangered Species	Pollution	

CODMAN SQUARE

MAY – – 1993

Cover photo: AP/Wide World Photos

Library of Congress Cataloging-in-Publication Data
Bernards, Neal, 1963-
     Elections : locating the author's main idea / by Neal Bernards ;
curriculum consultant, JoAnne Buggey.
          p. cm. — (Opposing viewpoints juniors)
     Includes bibliographical references and index..
     Summary: Presents differing views on the importance and
fairness of American elections, our primary system, and the role
of the media. Includes critical thinking activities.
     ISBN 1-56510-022-0 (acid free paper)
     1. Elections—United States—Juvenile literature. 2. Press and
politics—United States—Juvenile literature. 3. Critical thinking—
Juvenile literature. I. Buggey, JoAnne. II. Title. III. Series.
     JK1978.B47 1992
     324.973—dc20
                                                          92-21793
                                                          CIP

No part of this book may be reproduced or used in any other form or
by any other means, electrical, mechanical, or otherwise, including, but
not limited to, photocopy, recording, or any information storage and
retrieval system, without prior written permission from the publisher.

Copyright 1992 by Greenhaven Press, Inc.

CONTENTS

THE PURPOSE OF
THIS BOOK

An Introduction to
Opposing Viewpoints

When people disagree, it is hard to figure out who is right. You may decide one person is right just because the person is your friend or a relative. But this is not a very good reason to agree or disagree with someone. It is better if you try to understand why these people disagree. On what main points do they differ? Read or listen to each person's argument carefully. Separate the facts and opinions that each person presents. Finally, decide which argument best matches what you think. This process, examining an argument without emotion, is part of what critical thinking is all about.

This is not easy. Many things make it hard to understand and form opinions. People's values, ages, and experiences all influence the way they think. This is why learning to read and think critically is an invaluable skill.

Opposing Viewpoints Juniors books will help you learn and practice skills to improve your ability to read critically. By reading opposing views on an issue, you will become familiar with methods people use to attempt to convince you that their point of view is right. And you will learn to separate the authors' opinions from the facts they present.

Each Opposing Viewpoints Juniors book focuses on one critical thinking skill that will help you judge the views presented. Some of these skills are telling fact from opinion, recognizing propaganda techniques, and locating and analyzing the main idea. These skills will allow you to examine opposing viewpoints more easily. The viewpoints are placed in a running debate and are always placed with the pro view first.

Locating the Author's Main Idea

Authors include many ideas in their writing. But each sentence, each paragraph, and even each book they write should contain one main idea. For example, the main idea of this book is that America's elections are a point of debate.

Locating the author's main idea, whether it is within the sentence, paragraph, or entire piece of writing, is a basic reading skill. It is important because it allows readers to identify the theme of an author's writing. It also allows readers to understand the main point an author is trying to make about the theme.

In this Opposing Viewpoints Juniors book, you will be asked to analyze specific paragraphs to locate the main idea. Sometimes the main idea is placed at the beginning of the paragraph. Sometimes it is placed somewhere within the paragraph, or even at the end. For example:

> Oil producers have tapped most of the world's oil reserves for use by people in developed countries. They have also taken much of the world's natural gas and coal for use in power plants. If people are not forced to conserve soon, the world's natural resources will be gone in 100 years.

The main idea of this paragraph is placed at the end. It is that the world's resources are running out.

When you begin reading the paragraph, you might think the first sentence is the main idea. If it is, then the other sentences in the paragraph will support it in some way. They might explain the idea more specifically or give examples or reasons.

Read sentence two. Does it do any of these things? No. In fact, sentence two is very much like sentence one. Sentence two even says *also*, which suggests that the two sentences are giving two ideas about the same topic.

Now read the last sentence. It is a general statement about the world's resources, while the first two are specific examples of this. The last sentence in this paragraph is the topic sentence. The first two sentences support the last one.

If you outlined this paragraph, it would look like this:

1. If people are not forced to conserve soon, the world's natural resources will be gone in 100 years.
   A. (Example 1) Oil producers have tapped most of the world's oil reserves for use by people in developed countries.
   B. (Example 2) They have also taken much of the world's natural gas and coal for use in power plants.

Most paragraphs can be outlined in this way. By reading a paragraph carefully, you should be able to tell which sentence presents the main idea and which sentences explain or support it in some way. Outlining the paragraph may help you figure this out.

We asked two students to write one paragraph each in which they state their main ideas about America's elections. Examine the following viewpoints to locate the main ideas.

Voting can make a difference.

I think all Americans should vote because we all can make a difference. Because our government is a democracy, everyone needs to participate if the system is going to work. By voting, people can change the government. Voters can help get laws passed, get good people elected, and tell the government how to spend our tax money.

When Americans avoid voting or think that voting isn't important, it's terrible for the whole country. Then fewer people have a say in government. This might mean candidates will be elected that the majority of the people don't like. I don't think Americans should let that happen.

Voting does not make a difference.

Voting doesn't matter. The same people get elected over and over. Nothing ever changes because the rich and powerful are in control. They give the money for campaigns, so they decide who runs for office. Long before a candidate runs, he has already been bought by special interest groups and wealthy supporters. That's why we have so few choices today. My parents say that they are really discouraged because there is so little difference between the political candidates. Voting doesn't matter because we don't get to vote for anyone who has new or different ideas.

ANALYZING THE
SAMPLE VIEWPOINTS

Julie and Jeremy have very different opinions about America's elections. Each presents one main idea in his or her viewpoint.

Julie:
MAIN IDEA

Voting can make a difference.

Jeremy:
MAIN IDEA

Voting does not make a difference.

Both Julie and Jeremy placed their main ideas at the beginning of their statements.

As you continue to read through the viewpoints in this book, remember to look for the main idea of the specified paragraph.

CHAPTER 1

PREFACE: Are America's Elections Fair?

In the United States, two political parties are dominant: the Democratic party and the Republican party. Each party selects candidates to run for office, raises money for elections, and helps coordinate campaigns. The federal government gives each party $65.5 million every election year to pay for campaign costs. Whether this federal support of the two-party system is fair is a hotly contested issue. Many Americans believe the system discourages third-party candidates because they do not receive these monies. Third-party candidates must also fulfill lots of cumbersome requirements to run. Third-party presidential candidate Ross Perot discovered these barriers during his 1992 campaign. Perot was required to fulfill different requirements in all 50 states to get on the ballot since he ran as neither a Republican nor a Democrat.

Many voters also argue that the two parties do not fully represent the many types of people in the United States, especially minorities, women, and the poor. They believe elections favor male candidates from privileged backgrounds who were educated in fields such as law and business. These men have a hard time sympathizing with factory workers, farmers, blue-collar laborers, and women. Many people contend that the electoral system favors and reinforces a privileged white male upper class.

Others disagree and counter that America's elections are fair and open. Robert Kuttner, a political writer for the *New Republic*, writes, "The idea that everybody gets to participate in elections is the most wonderful thing about democracy." All adult citizens, except prisoners and convicted felons, can register to vote, and all candidates who follow the rules are allowed to run. No official barriers exist because of race, sex, religion, or political ideas. Supporters of America's elections point out that in countries like Iraq, Libya, and Cuba, citizens cannot select their government. The United States, they maintain, holds the fairest elections possible.

The authors in this chapter present their arguments on whether America's elections are fair. Read each viewpoint carefully and answer the questions in the margin. You will be asked to locate the authors' main ideas.

Editor's Note: The author of the following viewpoint argues that America's elections are the fairest in the world. He maintains that all citizens have an equal chance to run for office and to vote for the candidates of their choice. Read the viewpoint carefully and answer the questions in the margin.

The main idea of this paragraph is stated in the first sentence.

The main idea of this paragraph is that Americans are free to choose their leaders.

What is the main idea of this paragraph?

The democratic elections held in the United States are the fairest in the world. No other country has a longer or more respected history of free elections than the United States. From 1776 to the present, Americans have continuously elected candidates to office. This unrivaled accomplishment has made the American electoral process a model for other nations to follow.

Citizens in the United States are assured by law and custom the right to freely choose their leaders. Citizens are not forced to vote a certain way or even to vote at all. Voting is treated as a private affair. Voter decisions are kept secret to protect them from others who may disagree with how they vote.

American voters can choose among candidates from many political parties, including Communists, Libertarians, Democrats, Republicans, and independents. Many candidates run for each office. During presidential elections, ten to fifteen candidates are generally listed on the ballot. The only limit for certain positions is a minimum age requirement, a filing fee, or a certain number of signatures on a petition. This large number of choices does not exist in many countries. In China, for example, politicians often run unopposed. Or voters are forced to choose between two people from the same party. This type of election, without competition, is unfair. In America, competition is keen.

BLACK POLITICIANS GIVEN A FAIR CHANCE

Black Membership in State Legislatures, 1987				
State	Total number of legislators	Black legislators	% Black legislators	% Black population
Pennsylvania	253	18	7.1	8.0
Michigan	148	17	11.5	11.9
Missouri	197	14	7.1	9.0
Ohio	132	12	9.1	9.0
California	120	8	6.7	7.0
Nevada	60	3	5.0	6.0

Source: *Black Elected Officials* (Washington, D.C.: The Joint Center for Political Studies, 1987).

The American government enforces the rights of voters by making sure they are not discriminated against on the basis of race, religion, political views, or language. In fact, Matthew Cooper of the *Washington Monthly* notes that one in three black mayors are elected in white majority towns. This proves that America's elections do not discriminate by race. If they did, minorities would never get elected in mostly white areas. States such as California avoid language discrimination by printing ballots in English, Spanish, and Chinese so everyone can vote. This ensures that everyone has a fair chance to pick their leaders.

An interesting fact about America's elections is that no one, not even losing candidates, complains about corrupt elections. Losers may ask for a recount. Or they may claim that their opponents used unfair campaign tactics. But they rarely complain that the election was rigged. Robert Goldberg, a political analyst, writes in *Elections American Style* that "electoral fraud is not a clear or present danger to practical democracy in most parts of the U.S. today." While election fraud was rampant around the time of the Civil War, the process has been reformed. Strict rules now govern elections. Voters cannot vote more than once, and tight security guarantees that ballot boxes cannot be stolen.

Americans are happy with their government. This proves that elections are fair. Even though millions of Americans may disagree with certain political policies, they have never attempted to overthrow the government. Americans believe they can speak their minds peacefully through voting. In countries like El Salvador and the Philippines, where unfair elections are commonplace, many people take up arms because they know their votes will not be counted. In the United States, voters know that if they disagree with the government, they can vote current officeholders out of office. They trust the system to work.

America's elections are the fairest in the world. The Constitution and state voting laws ensure that they stay that way. All citizens get an equal chance to run for office, to vote for the candidates they like, or to simply not vote at all.

Do the sentences toward the end of the paragraph support the main idea? Why or why not?

The main idea of this viewpoint is that America's elections are fair. Does this paragraph support the main idea? Why or why not?

The main idea of this paragraph comes at the end. What is it?

Voting and fairness

Why does the author think America's elections are fair? What evidence does he give to support his argument? Do you think the author's argument is convincing? Why or why not?

Editor's Note: In the following viewpoint, the author writes that America's elections are unfair because they favor wealthy, powerful candidates. The author argues that candidates who are poor or who do not have connections cannot win when running against Democratic and Republican politicians. Note the author's main idea in each paragraph.

The main idea of this viewpoint is that America's elections are unfair because politicians do not represent the public. Does the information in this paragraph support the main idea? Why or why not?

On the surface, America's elections look as if they are fair and just, but they are not. Just look at the politicians who get elected. Anyone can see that discrimination occurs in our "democracy." These politicians are not representative of the people of the United States.

Most politicians who get elected are rich and powerful, while the people they represent are not. Politicians themselves have commented on this fact. New York senator Patrick Moynihan notes that over half of the members of the U.S. Senate are millionaires. Congress members as a whole are in the top 10 to 15 percent of the nation's income scale. These people cannot represent the majority of Americans because they do not understand common people's problems. The wealthy do not know what it is like to be hungry, jobless, homeless, or on welfare. They are not sympathetic to the daily pressures of having to pay rent, buy clothes, and feed a family on a small income. Government officials need to understand the concerns of the people they represent.

The U.S. House of Representatives is no better than the Senate. Over 50 percent of House members have law degrees. Lawyers tend to be middle- to upper-class white men. This contrasts with a nation whose lower class is growing and whose number of minority citizens is increasing. While there are many lawyers in the United States, they do not account for half the country's population. This is unfair representation. Though the concerns of lawyers are well represented, the concerns of most others are not. Why do not farmers, carpenters, housewives, and service people get elected? Because the electoral process discriminates against them.

Common people are not in office because they do not have the time or money to campaign. Running for office can be very expensive. The average U.S. Senate campaign now costs $3 million. This amount is beyond the means of all but the wealthiest people. Even raising that much money from donors takes power and influence that most Americans do not have. The result? Only political candidates with name recognition or prestige (wealthy business leaders, lawyers, and entertainers) can afford to run for office. Many current leaders are good examples. Palm Springs mayor Sonny Bono was an entertainer. And of course, former president Ronald Reagan was an actor long before he entered politics.

The two-party system is another reason that America's elections remain unfair. The Democrats and Republicans have a lock on every state and national election. Third-party candidates or independents do not have a chance. Political observers say that John Anderson, who ran for president in 1980 as an independent, did very well in the election. Anderson got only 6 percent of the vote, nowhere near enough to have an impact.

America's elections cannot be fair when only two political party platforms are presented to voters, especially when those platforms are so similar. Political expert Michael Parenti describes the Democrats and Republicans as "fraternal twins" because they are so much alike. They are both huge, well-financed organizations that exist to support capitalism and the current system of government. Because the Democrats and Republicans dominate the election process, voters feel as though they are throwing their votes away if they select Socialists, Libertarians, Green party candidates, or nonaligned representatives.

DUNAGIN'S PEOPLE

"YOU HAVE AN EXCELLENT RECORD, SENATOR! IT WOULD TAKE AN EXTRAORDINARY OPPONENT OR $3.5 MILLION TO UNSEAT YOU!"

Reprinted with special permission of © 1987 North American Syndicate, Inc.

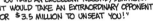

The author's main idea in this paragraph may be a little difficult to locate. Read it carefully and decide which sentence best expresses the main idea.

What is the main idea of this paragraph?

Locate the author's main idea in this paragraph.

Another point of view

What is the author's main idea throughout the viewpoint? After reading both viewpoints, which author do you find more convincing? Why?

The following paragraphs each contain one main idea. Below each paragraph are three sentences, one of which best expresses the main idea of the paragraph. Read each paragraph and circle the sentence that best expresses the main idea. Remember to read the paragraphs carefully. Many sentences may be related to the main idea, but you must choose the one that *best* expresses it. You may wish to outline these paragraphs before you choose.

Example: Running an election campaign costs a lot of money, especially for television advertisements. Many politicians drop from races because they run out of money. For this reason, elections favor the rich. They can spend their own money and get additional support from their wealthy friends.

    a) Television advertising is expensive.
    b) The poor cannot win elections.
    c) America's elections favor the rich.

The answer is c)—America's elections favor the rich. This sentence tells us the main idea the author is discussing. Sentence a) supports the main idea. Sentence b) is not discussed in the paragraph.

1. Senator Paul Wellstone of Minnesota won a surprising victory over Rudy Boschwitz in 1990. Before becoming senator, Wellstone was a political science professor at a small college. This political outsider successfully campaigned by touring the state on a broken-down bus. Wellstone's victory proves that America's elections are fair and open to all.

   a) Political outsiders can win elections.
   b) America's elections are fair.
   c) Wellstone beat Boschwitz in 1990.

2. Some nations have had the same leaders for more than twenty years. Fidel Castro of Cuba and Moammar Khadafy of Libya both rose to power through military takeovers. They do not permit free elections. Americans should be thankful for the right to vote. Not everyone gets to enjoy that freedom.

   a) Americans should be thankful for the right to vote.
   b) Castro and Khadafy do not hold free elections.
   c) Not all people are free.

3. Third-party candidates have a difficult time getting elected. They do not enjoy the support of a large, well-organized party. They do not get automatic media coverage at their meetings. And most people know little of their politics. Third-party candidates fight a constant, uphill battle to get elected.

   a) Third-party candidates do not get media coverage.
   b) It is difficult for third-party candidates to get elected.
   c) Few people know the politics of alternative parties.

CHAPTER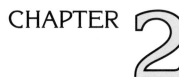

PREFACE: Does Voting Matter?

In the 1988 presidential election between George Bush and Michael Dukakis, 91,602,291 Americans voted. That may seem like a lot until one realizes that 91,050,000 registered voters did not vote. The 50.15 percent voter turnout rate was the lowest in sixty-four years, falling nearly 20 percent short of voter turnout in most other industrialized countries.

Many people argue that this low turnout is due to voter apathy: Many Americans claim that voting is useless because they cannot change the government. Bob Avakian, in his book *Democracy: Can't We Do Better Than That?*, writes, "There never has been and never will be a revolution through the ballot box." Avakian states that the government and big business would never allow true change to come through voting. Instead, he argues, they would alter election rules to guarantee their power against angry voters. Avakian believes many Americans refuse to vote since they know radical change is not possible through elections.

Millions of other voters disagree and prove it by voting in every election. Most believe that their votes count. In their book *Few Are Chosen*, Robert E. DeClerico and Eric M. Uslaner ask, "Why should anyone vote? There are four reasons: (1) voting is what democracy is all about; (2) the entire system would collapse if no one voted; (3) voting is the only way that you can be sure that your voice will be heard; and (4) voting is simply important in itself." People like DeClerico and Uslaner believe that by working together, voters can make a difference in their government.

The authors of the following viewpoints debate the issue of whether voting is important. Locate the author's main idea in each viewpoint and answer the margin questions.

Editor's Note: In the following viewpoint, the author argues that voting remains the best way for private citizens to influence their government. He writes that political action committees (PACs), special interest groups, and large campaign donors still bow to the will of public opinion.

What evidence does the author give to support his main idea that voting is a powerful tool?

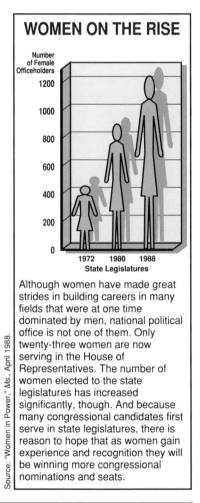

WOMEN ON THE RISE

Number
of Female
Officeholders

1200
1000
800
600
400
200
0

1972   1980   1988
State Legislatures

Although women have made great strides in building careers in many fields that were at one time dominated by men, national political office is not one of them. Only twenty-three women are now serving in the House of Representatives. The number of women elected to the state legislatures has increased significantly, though. And because many congressional candidates first serve in state legislatures, there is reason to hope that as women gain experience and recognition they will be winning more congressional nominations and seats.

Source: "Women in Power," *Ms.*, April 1988.

The main idea in this paragraph is that one vote can make a difference. Do the other sentences support this idea?

Voting is the foundation of American democracy. It is the most effective tool for social change. Voters can elect leaders, recall officials, cut taxes, raise money, and tell government how to run the country. That voting is the most important tool for private citizens to influence their government can readily be seen throughout American history. Voters banned alcohol during Prohibition, for example. They voted unpopular president Jimmy Carter out of office in 1980.

Many people decry the fact that PACs and big corporations have money to influence legislation. But no amount of money can overcome the will of the people. For example, in 1990 a building contractor wanted to build a group home for emotionally disturbed youths in the Minneapolis suburb of Brooklyn Center. Many of the local governing bodies, including the city council and mayor, had approved the project. However, neighbors of the proposed project objected. They organized themselves and voiced their concerns at a city zoning committee meeting. Strong community reaction caused the zoning committee to vote against approving the project.

If Americans do not like the system or their politicians, they have only themselves to blame. The people *are* the government in a democracy. Instead of taking this responsibility, however, most people stay home, complaining that their votes do not matter. When change does not happen, they throw up their hands and say, "See?" That is simple laziness. If you hate the government, stop complaining long enough to get out and vote. As Mary O'Connell, a community activist in Chicago, writes, "Voting is how decisions get made. Not to participate is to be at best foolish (because your claim is not heard) and at worst irresponsible." O'Connell believes that American voters have the power to change the future of the country.

One vote may not seem like much in an election with millions of voters, but it can make the difference between winning and losing. Many state and national elections have been decided by a handful of votes. In the 1960 presidential election between Richard Nixon and John Kennedy, for example, Kennedy won by only 112,803, even though 69 million votes were cast. In fact, had only 15,000 more people voted for Nixon in the key states of Hawaii, Illinois, Missouri, and South Carolina, Nixon would have won the electoral college vote and the presidency. Kennedy's victory proves that every vote counts.

© Mike Peters. Rerpinted with permission.

If voting does not matter, why did so many disadvantaged groups in America work so hard to attain it? They know it is important because they fought long and hard for the right. Women struggled for decades before finally gaining the right to vote in 1920. African-Americans were allowed to vote after the Civil War, but various states took their voting privileges away. The Civil Rights movement of the late 1950s and early 1960s was largely fueled by the need to restore the vote to all African-Americans. These long-suffering groups fought for the right to vote because it is a powerful tool. No vote means no representation. African-Americans and women have effectively used their votes to put candidates in office who represent their interests.

If nothing else, people can use their votes as a way to send a message to the existing government. In the presidential primaries of 1992, voters protested the lack of choice and lack of action among favored candidates. Many Democrats supported former California governor Jerry Brown and his message that American politics needed new faces and new solutions, not more mainstream candidates. Likewise, many Republican voters voiced their dissatisfaction with President George Bush by casting ballots for Patrick Buchanan. These protest votes shocked both Democratic and Republican party leaders into promising to change their platforms. These elections proved that voting produces change.

The author's main idea may be more difficult to locate in this paragraph. Read it carefully to determine the point the author is trying to make.

Which sentence best expresses the main idea of this paragraph?

Power of the people

What examples does the author give to support his main idea that voting makes a difference in the political process? How does this contrast with the next author's main idea? After reading both viewpoints, which side would you support? Why?

Editor's Note: The author of the following viewpoint argues that voting is useless. He maintains that voters cannot make a difference in a system dominated by political action committees and special interest groups.

The main idea of this viewpoint is located in the first paragraph. Which sentence best expresses it?

This paragraph contains many ideas. What point do you think the author is trying to make?

Money makes American politics tick. Elected leaders may wield political clout and citizens may possess the power of the vote, but when it comes to elections, campaign donors have the upper hand. Campaign donors are the ones who truly influence America's elections. They control who runs and who wins. Individual voters simply have no impact. The voices of private citizens are drowned out by the overwhelming influence of well-organized and monied lobbying groups such as the National Rifle Association.

Many of these lobbying groups are political action committees (PACs) that are set up by corporations, unions, and other organizations. PACs collect money from individuals to give to political candidates. In return for this money, PACs demand favors from candidates once they reach office. For example, tobacco growers have a powerful lobby in Washington, D.C. Despite the known health effects of smoking, tobacco growers continue to receive money from the federal government for growing their crops. Candidates who receive contributions from the tobacco lobby are expected to vote to continue government subsidies of tobacco crops. The influence and number of such PACs continue to grow. In 1974 there were only 608 PACs. Today there are over 4,000.

The influence of PACs makes voting meaningless. Individual voters are unable to have their concerns voiced by today's candidates. Instead, the candidates pander to the people who will give them money. As former senator Gary Hart of Colorado writes, "It seems the

WHO DO THEY REPRESENT?

		The Senate	The House
100th	Business & Banking	68 (68%)	242 (56%)
	Law	25 (25%)	159 (37%)
91st	Business & Banking	62 (62%)	184 (42.3%)
	Law	28 (28%)	142 (32.6%)

OCCUPATIONAL BACKGROUND OF MEMBERS OF CONGRESS, 91ST AND 100TH CONGRESS COMPARED

Source: *Congressional Quarterly Weekly Report* (1987, Nov. 15, p. 2985, (1969, Jan. 3, p. 46).

only group without a well-heeled PAC is the average citizen, whose demands the PACs have drowned out."

Politicians listen to PACs because the election system is rigged. Though candidates need votes to get elected, they first need money to get votes. The $100 million PACs "donate" to candidates each year is a powerful tool. It allows the favored candidates to attract the public's attention through advertising and by mailings. Elections are decided before the average citizen even has a chance to decide who to vote for.

The power and influence of PACs can be seen in areas such as gun control. A majority of Americans support tougher gun control laws than now exist. According to a March 1991 Gallup poll, 87 percent of Americans favor a seven-day waiting period for handguns. However, less than half the states have passed a waiting period law because of the National Rifle Association (NRA). The NRA spends millions of dollars each year to defeat gun control laws and unseat the legislators who propose them. The NRA has been extremely effective in gaining its own objectives while thwarting the desires of the general public. It is a prime example of how PACs, with their money and political influence, make voting useless.

What is the main idea of this paragraph? Do the other sentences in the paragraph support the main idea? Why or why not?

Voting does not really change anything. Most citizens are too uninvolved to vote for change, so they just vote the same people into office every year. For example, in the 1988 election for the U.S. House of Representatives, 402 of 408 incumbents were reelected. Incumbents are politicians already in office who must run against challengers. Ninety-eight percent of all House members were reelected. This means that very little changed during the long, expensive campaign of 1988. Even politicians who ran up the deficit and misspent government money were put right back into office. People just do not pay any attention when they vote. They simply vote for a recognizable name. Once elected, politicians are hard to get out of office. The people who want to change things remain few and far between. Since, in a democracy, the majority rules, the minority gives up.

The founders of the United States would be appalled at their "democracy." Large, wealthy political organizations and corporations hold the power. Government of the people, by the people, and for the people is a well-turned phrase, but it is hopelessly outdated today.

POLITICIANS WHO GET REELECTED

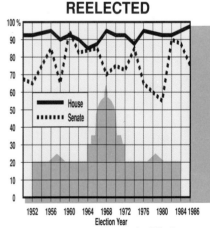

Sources: Barbara Hinckley, *Congressional Elections.* [Washington, D.C.: Congressional Quarterly Press, 1981], p. 39; and Norman J. Orstein et al., *Vital Statistics on Congress,* 1987-1988 [Washington, D.C.: Congressional Quarterly Press, 1987], pp. 56-57.

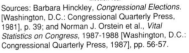

Voting and PACs

Who does the author believe holds power in the United States? Why does he say this makes voting useless? Do you agree with the author? Why or why not?

SKILL **Selecting the Main Idea**

The following paragraphs are taken from the viewpoints in this chapter. Each paragraph contains one main idea. Below each paragraph are spaces to outline the paragraph by stating the main idea along with the supporting ideas. Read carefully and outline each paragraph below. Compare your answers with those of your classmates.

Example: The founders of the United States would be appalled at their "democracy." Large, wealthy political organizations and corporations hold the power. Government of the people, by the people, and for the people is a well-turned phrase, but it is hopelessly outdated today.

Main idea: The founders would be appalled at democracy today.

Supporting ideas: Government of the people, by the people, and for the people is an outdated phrase.
Large, wealthy organizations hold power.

1. Voting is the foundation of American democracy. It is the most effective tool for social change. Voters can elect leaders, recall officials, cut taxes, raise money, and tell government how to run the country.

Main idea:

Supporting ideas:

2. A vote by the average citizen means nothing when PACs give out more than $100 million each election year. While candidates need votes to get elected, they need money to get votes. Therefore, candidates listen to wealthy PACs while ignoring the interests of individual voters.

Main idea:

Supporting ideas:

3. Voters create the government in a democracy. For all the talk about the influence of PACs, money, and special interest groups, voters remain the most powerful group in America. No politician, not even the president, is immune from public opinion.

Main idea:

Supporting ideas:

PREFACE: Does the Primary System Work?

Presidential nominees are selected through a series of elections called primaries and state-wide meetings called caucuses. Both the Democrats and Republicans use primaries to select their nominees. The long primary process causes unpopular candidates to drop out of the race, reducing the field of contenders from many to few. Primaries are unique because the public directly votes for their candidate of choice. The presidential primaries start in January of each election year in Iowa and New Hampshire. They end in the summer with the Democratic and the Republican national conventions. There, candidates receive their party's nomination.

The primary system enjoys popular support because it gives citizens a direct say in choosing a president. Donald L. Robinson, a professor of government at Smith College in Massachusetts, writes, "No other nation in the world has chosen its candidates for leader by a direct election." In many European democracies, such as in England and Germany, political party leaders choose the candidates for prime minister or president. Voters in these countries have little say over who is selected to run for the highest office in each of their nations.

However, many political observers, including NBC News commentator John Chancellor, argue that the primary system produces poor candidates. They criticize candidates' negative advertising and the media's superficial coverage. Chancellor writes, "Every four years (during the primaries), the American voter is subjected to ten months of banal hucksterism, tasteless advertising, and shallow rhetoric." Some commentators also question the quick narrowing of the primary field. A candidate who loses early primaries may withdraw. This means that voters in large states with later primaries, such as California, are left with fewer choices. Instead of primaries, Chancellor and journalist William Pfaff contend that political experts should nominate candidates.

The authors of the following viewpoints debate the effectiveness of the primary system.

Editor's Note: The author of the following viewpoint believes the primary system is the best method of choosing presidential candidates. He maintains that the long, difficult process forces candidates to prove their leadership skills and gives the public a chance to examine their political views.

Which sentence contains the main idea, the first or the last? Why?

Locate the main idea in this paragraph.

When a job candidate applies for a job, he or she must impress a potential employer during an interview. The potential employer uses the interview as a way to judge the candidate's qualifications, personality, and fit with the job opening. Primaries allow voters to judge candidates in much the same way that a job interview allows an employer to judge a potential employee. The primary system is an effective way to select a president because politicians must outline their specific proposals before the public and media.

Primaries force candidates to prove themselves to the public. Candidates must answer tough questions and face important issues. They must explain exactly what their policies are and how they hope to make them work. Reporters continually challenge candidates on their political stances, personal inconsistencies, and their track records, if they hold other offices. The debates and speeches during a primary let the public know what a candidate thinks and what he or she will do if elected.

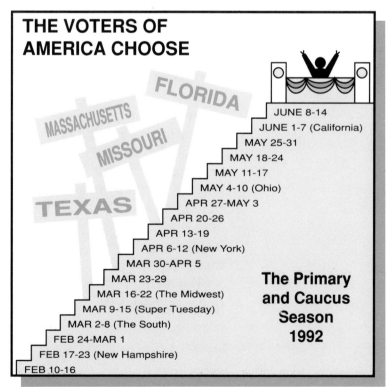

THE VOTERS OF AMERICA CHOOSE

JUNE 8-14
JUNE 1-7 (California)
MAY 25-31
MAY 18-24
MAY 11-17
MAY 4-10 (Ohio)
APR 27-MAY 3
APR 20-26
APR 13-19
APR 6-12 (New York)
MAR 30-APR 5
MAR 23-29
MAR 16-22 (The Midwest)
MAR 9-15 (Super Tuesday)
MAR 2-8 (The South)
FEB 24-MAR 1
FEB 17-23 (New Hampshire)
FEB 10-16

MASSACHUSETTS
FLORIDA
MISSOURI
TEXAS

The Primary and Caucus Season 1992

The skills needed to win during the long, grueling primary process are the same skills needed to run the country. The simple fact is that no better process exists to choose our presidents. As Everett Carl Ladd of the *Christian Science Monitor* writes, "No convincing practical alternative has been found." If primaries were shortened, or candidates selected differently, the public might not get a chance to thoroughly examine those who want to become president.

Other systems of choosing leaders that are used in many Western European countries are not as democratic. In Britain, for example, voters do not vote for candidates, but for the party they would like to see in power. The party with the most votes chooses the prime minister. The British Labor and Tory parties do not choose a prime minister on the basis of public acceptance. They reward politicians who have been loyal to the party or who are popular with their colleagues. This means that a person could become prime minister and yet be hated by the people.

In the United States, citizens get to vote directly for their government officials. It is not the Democratic or Republican party leaders who choose the president, but the people themselves. This allows voters to select leaders who appeal to them. It makes the public directly responsible for putting their leaders in power.

The primary system gives every politician an equal chance. It allows politicians from all over the United States a chance to win. Jimmy Carter, for example, was a little-known governor from Georgia before he became president in 1976. The election of former actor Ronald Reagan was equally surprising. The primaries gave voters an opportunity to show their support for these political outsiders. Had it been left to party leaders, neither Carter nor Reagan would have been nominated. Instead, party leaders would have chosen candidates well known to them—candidates who had spent their careers inside Washington, D.C., pandering to party leaders. Through primaries, voters let it be known if they want a change from insider politics.

Primaries work. They allow almost any well-organized politician a chance to run for president while quickly weeding out those who are not serious or whom the public does not want. The primary system remains the best means of selecting our presidential hopefuls.

MARATHON RUNNER

© Graham/Rothco. Reprinted with permission.

What is the main idea of this paragraph? Do you agree with it? Explain your answer.

This paragraph describes the British electoral system. Which sentence do you think contains the main idea?

The main idea of the viewpoint is that primaries help select the best candidates. Does this paragraph support this main idea? Why or why not?

Presidents and primaries

Why does the author support a long primary process? Do you agree with his argument? Why or why not? Name two character traits the author believes primaries help candidates to develop.

Editor's Note: In the following viewpoint, the author contends that primary elections do not produce good candidates. Instead, he argues, primaries produce shallow politicians who appeal to the public while revealing little of themselves. The author believes that political professionals and party leaders should select presidential candidates.

Sex scandals. Draft dodging. Drug use. Tax returns. Are these tabloid topics? Hardly. These and other sensational topics have become the focus of presidential primaries. The primary system has become so warped and twisted that it no longer serves a useful purpose. It does nothing more than reward political survivors and fence-sitters while discouraging candidates who offer innovation and change.

What is the main idea of this paragraph? Do the remaining sentences support it?

Primaries do not work because they promote shallow politics. Rather than expressing views, candidates vie for popularity by staging a variety of publicity stunts that are an embarrassment to American politics. Candidates milk cows, work on assembly lines, tour hospitals, and eat chili at state fairs. During these events, candidates mindlessly mouth slogans and empty rhetoric. They desperately try to avoid saying anything of substance. This style of campaigning favors politicians who look good on television while discouraging those with something to say. People like Ronald Reagan, often labeled "The Great Communicator," flourish under this system, while thoughtful politicians like Paul Tsongas of Massachusetts suffer.

Barely one-half of the nation's voting age population (50.1 percent) voted in the November 1988 presidential election. But the only state where turnout came even close to that level in 1990 was Louisiana—where candidates often are elected in the primary, obviating a general election altogether.

The accompanying chart gives 1990 turnout rates for states where both parties had candidates for statewide office (governor, senator, or at-large House member). Wherever possible, turnout rates are based on ballots cast in gubernatorial races, traditionally the focal point of voter interest in midterm elections.

PRIMARY APATHY

Primary Turnout
(as percentage of voting age population)

	Total Vote	Dems.	GOP		Total Vote	Dems.	GOP
Louisiana	45	—	—	Rhode Island	23	22	1
Wyoming	36	13	23	Idaho	22	6	16
Alaska	34	16	18	Minnesota	22	12	10
Arkansas	32	27	5	North Dakota	22	13	9
Montana	32	17	15	California	20	11	9
Massachusetts	32	23	9	Nevada	19	10	9
Oklahoma	31	23	8	Texas	19	12	7
Nebraska	30	14	16	Florida	17	10	7
Hawaii	29	24	5	North Carolina	17	13	4
Alabama	28	24	4	Maryland	16	12	4
Kansas	26	9	17	New Hampshire	15	5	10
Georgia	24	21	3	Pennsylvania	15	9	6
New Mexico	24	17	7	Kentucky	14	11	3
Oregon	24	12	12	Vermont	14	4	10
Arizona	23	9	14				

Source: Congressional Quarterly Weekly Report, October 20, 1990.

The primaries are a burden to American society. John Chancellor, a commentator for NBC News, writes, "Presidential campaigns last too long, cost too much, and too often produce poor candidates." Primaries waste time and money. Candidates who hold office while campaigning neglect their work so they can give speeches and kiss babies from coast to coast. They spend anywhere from $1 million to $10 million trying to gain the public's favor. These disadvantages are not outweighed by quality results. Usually, the public ends up with two tired politicians whom few want to see as president.

The primary process makes a mockery of democracy. Instead of allowing everyone to choose, primaries place undue emphasis on the election results in the tiny states that hold their primaries early. The voters of New Hampshire and Iowa have an unfair influence simply because they vote first. Candidates who do poorly in these states often drop out of the race, leaving the rest of the country with fewer choices. In essence, primaries are only democratic for those people lucky enough to vote early. Californians, with one-eighth of the country's population, have little say in selecting presidential candidates because their primary falls "late," in June.

The job of picking presidential candidates should be left to the experts. Let party leaders and political pros select the best person for the job. They know the politicians, their histories, and their ability to handle the pressures of leadership. Fellow politicians understand who is effective and who is not. The public only understands what it sees on television. John Chancellor states that voters would be better served by abolishing primary elections and party caucuses. He writes, "There is nothing in the Constitution that requires primary elections. The best reform would be to let party professionals and elected officials choose the party's candidate for the fall campaign."

Primaries do not produce the best candidates. They produce politicians who try to appeal to everyone at once. Once the primaries are abandoned, the election process will become much more meaningful.

Which sentence best expresses the author's main idea in this paragraph?

No one sentence seems to state the author's main idea. What point is he trying to make in this paragraph?

What is the main idea of the entire viewpoint? Does this paragraph support the main idea or does it present another idea? Explain your answer.

"THAT ONE'S FOR ELECTION YEARS..."

John Trever. Reprinted with permission.

The underside of politics

What proof does the author offer that primaries last too long and cost too much? Why does he argue that they are undemocratic?
After reading both viewpoints, which side do you support? Why?

Locating the Main Idea in Editorial
Cartoons

Throughout this book, you have seen cartoons that illustrate the ideas in the viewpoints. Cartoonists use humor to present their opinion on an issue. Cartoonists, like writers, express a main idea in their cartoons. Sometimes the main idea is obvious. At other times, a reader must observe the clues given in the words and illustrations to determine the main idea.

Look at the cartoon below. Why do you think the machine looks so complicated? What observations can you make about the machine? What does the machine produce? Based on your observations, what do you think is the main idea of the cartoon?

Don Wright. Reprinted with permission.

For further practice, look at the editorial cartoons in your daily newspaper. Try to decide what main idea the author is expressing in the cartoon.

CHAPTER

PREFACE: Should the Media Publicize Candidates' Private Lives?

If a politician does not appear on television, voters cannot hear about him or her. Television coverage is so vital, argue Stephen A. Salmore and Barbara G. Salmore, authors of the book *Candidates, Parties, and Campaigns*, that most candidates spend 60 percent of their campaign budgets on television advertising.

Although candidates seek media exposure, it can be disastrous if the coverage is harmful. Senator Gary Hart of Colorado lost his bid to become the Democratic candidate for president in 1988 when photos were published of him and a young model embracing aboard a yacht. NBC News commentator John Chancellor writes, "Hart destroyed his candidacy because of personal mistakes. Had he not stumbled, he might have won . . . his party's nomination." The media was quick to report Hart's stumble. Many question whether this kind of publicity is really necessary. They see the media as gossipmongers, digging up dirt for a good story.

Those in the media disagree with these criticisms. They justify their actions by arguing that a candidate's personal life tells a great deal about him or her. In the case of Gary Hart, for example, reporters hounded him about his reputation of being a lady's man. Hart challenged reporters to follow him to disprove the allegation. Reporters immediately confirmed that he did entertain other women. Voters were left wondering why Hart would make such a foolish challenge. His poor judgment became evident.

Much of the public, however, believes that the media goes too far in exposing a candidate's private life. Many argue that it is immaterial whether Arkansas governor Bill Clinton smoked marijuana in college or whether former California governor Jerry Brown allowed drug use to occur in the governor's mansion during his tenure. Syndicated columnist William Safire writes, "No public figure, not even a porno star, should have to bare his or her soul or take polygraph tests on personal morality as a condition of employment." Continued media exposure of candidates' private lives might keep good candidates from running for office.

The authors in this chapter debate what amount of coverage the media should give to candidates' private lives. There are no sidebar questions in these viewpoints to help you. You must read the viewpoints carefully to locate the main ideas and answer the questions at the end of the viewpoint.

ELECTIONS **27**

The media should publicize candidates' private lives

Editor's Note: In the following viewpoint, the author states that the media has a right to report all newsworthy events during campaigns, including politicians' private lives. Remember that there are no questions in this viewpoint to help you. Read the viewpoint closely and answer the focus box questions following it.

It is the media's job to report the news. If a candidate says that he does not cheat on his wife, but does, that is news. If a candidate supports military actions like the Gulf War, but he himself dodged the draft, that is news. The public needs this kind of campaign reporting. It helps voters to understand the candidates and it makes their voting decisions easier. The media has a right, even a duty, to publicize candidates' private lives.

Many charge that this focus on candidates' private lives obscures the issues. Since the media cannot report everything, they must sacrifice coverage of a candidate's policies to focus on what he or she did while in college. But the candidates' positions on the issues are not the news. Candidates rarely have anything new to say on issues. They just mouth what the public wants to hear. Stephen Salmore, a political science professor at Rutgers University, and Barbara Salmore, a professor of political science at Drew University, write, "Once a candidate's position on the issues is reported, it is not news unless it changes. On the other other hand, charges against other candidates, new poll results, and discord within the campaign are events that merit reporting." While many people may call this coverage mud slinging, the media are obligated to report these events because they are newsworthy.

Reprinted by permission: Tribune Media Services.

Besides, most revelations about a candidate's private life do little damage. Governor Bill Clinton of Arkansas survived charges of draft dodging, extramarital affairs, and golfing at an all-white country club to become the Democratic candidate for president in 1992. The American public can decide which accusations are important and which are not. Clinton's past did not seem relevant. Gary Hart's past, on the other hand, did. He was bounced from the primaries in 1988 because he claimed one thing and did another. His lack of judgment and self-control had to be pointed out by the media. Their reporting helped the public realize that Hart could not be trusted.

Americans should remember that no one forces politicians to run for office. These people choose to become public figures. Once they announce their candidacy, politicians know that they become fair game for the media. Their lives become public property. If they do not want their past analyzed, they should get out of politics. The media has every right to investigate politicians' pasts to see if their claims are true. Candidates will try to portray only the good sides of their personalities while sheltering the bad. The media's job is to show the whole person.

In the end, media scrutiny leads to better candidates. It tells the public if certain politicians can be trusted to keep their word or if they have a history of making promises they cannot keep. What if the media had kept David Duke's past a secret during his campaign for governor of Louisiana? The world would never have known about his history with the Ku Klux Klan. It would have been easy to accept Duke as a slick politician who believed in basic family values. Instead, the media exposed Duke for the racist that he was.

The public needs to know the background of their politicians. They cannot make informed voting decisions without knowing a candidate's past. It would be like marrying someone just after meeting them or buying a car without a test drive. The media provide a valuable service by publicizing a candidate's private life.

Asking the media to draw a line between what it should report and what it should not report would be disastrous. The media's duty is to report anything that seems newsworthy, including candidates' private lives. The public is best served when the media is allowed to do its job.

Private life in the public sector

How does the author define news? What point is he trying to make about media coverage of political campaigns?

According to the author, what is the media's role? How does that view relate to the author's main idea of the viewpoint?

Editor's Note: The author of the following viewpoint argues that the media does not have a right to publicize candidates' private lives. He states that they should report serious political issues. As in the previous viewpoint, carefully locate the main ideas and answer the focus box questions at the end.

The media cannot continue to tear candidates apart for personal mistakes. Otherwise, the country will be stuck with boring politicians who always play it safe. The media's snooping drives away quality candidates and encourages those who lead bland, uneventful lives. Bland politicians make for a bland government. The type of person America needs is a risk taker, one willing to stand for what he or she thinks is right. In order to attract this type of person, the media must stop invading the privacy of candidates' personal lives. The media should only report information that directly pertains to the election at hand.

Up until the 1960s, reporters and commentators were more selective in what they reported. Toward the end of his administration, for example, President Franklin Roosevelt could no longer walk by himself. He used a wheelchair much of the time. Reporters kept his frailty to themselves because they thought it was a personal matter. They also thought the public needed to believe in a strong leader during the difficult times of World War II. Similarly, during John F. Kennedy's tenure in office, the press did not report on his many affairs, including one with Marilyn Monroe. The press rightfully decided that these affairs did not have a bearing on his political decisions. The media respected a politician's right to privacy. The media should apply this same discretion today.

Joel Pett/*The Lexington Herald-Leader.* Reprinted with permission.

The media should learn that publicizing politicians' private lives can lead to many unfounded accusations. For instance, during the 1992 Democratic primary campaign, Jerry Brown accused Bill Clinton of illegally directing work to his wife's law firm. The charges, though unfounded, were reported. The tables turned on Brown later in the campaign. The *Los Angeles Times* printed accusations that while governor of California, Brown had parties where others used drugs. No reliable evidence was given to support the charge. The public learned nothing through either accusation except that the media are very willing to print any accusation suggesting scandal. Rather than serving the public, the media merely served to reveal themselves as gossip spreaders.

The media is so absorbed with digging up dirt that the public has little chance to find out what politicians think about important issues facing the government. Rather than finding out what candidates will do once in office, the media asks questions about drug use, army service, and sex life. This line of questioning violates candidates' privacy and ignores their qualifications for office.

Delving into candidates' private lives scares off qualified politicians. The prying drives away good candidates who know they may have a skeleton or two in their closet. Few people can hold up under the type of examination current candidates must endure. Everything from college papers to private friendships seem to be fair game. The media have gone too far. William Safire, a syndicated columnist in the *New York Times*, agrees and writes, "Privacy for candidates should stop where wealth and health begin. Tell us your holdings and show us your tax returns. But no public figure should have to bare his or her soul as a condition of employment."

The media would serve the public better by concentrating on issues and laying off the personal histories. Leave the gossip to the tabloids.

Four of the men who would never have been President under today's media scrutiny.

Paul Conrad, © 1992, Los Angeles Times. Reprinted with permission.

Lies and innuendos

According to the author, how does reporting on a candidate's private life hurt the election process? What is the author's main idea in the viewpoint?

After reading the two viewpoints, do you think the media should report on candidates' private lives? Why or why not?

CRITICAL THINKING 4 SKILL Developing the Main Idea

Below are ten statements. Each is related to the information you have read in these viewpoints. Choose one and make it the main idea of a paragraph you write.

Example: Topic idea: The media can influence close elections.

The media can influence close elections. How a candidate performs before the press can make the difference between winning and losing. For example, in 1960, presidential candidates Richard Nixon and John Kennedy held a live television debate. Nixon looked uncomfortable while Kennedy presented himself well. Many voters were influenced by Kennedy's cool appearance and riveting delivery. They voted for Kennedy, giving him a narrow victory over Nixon.

Main Ideas:

1. Voting is the duty of all Americans.

2. Elections favor celebrities and the wealthy.

3. Presidential candidates should be picked by politicians.

4. Low voter turnout proves that something is wrong with America's elections.

5. Primaries are the best way to select a president.

6. PACs have too much influence on elections.

7. America's elections are democratic.

8. The public has no right to know a candidate's private life.

9. Elections take too long and cost too much.

10. The media keep politicians honest.

FOR FURTHER READING

The author recommends the following periodicals for further research on the topic. Check the works consulted list that follows for further suggestions.

William L. Armstrong, "Campaign Reform: An Exercise in Cynicism," *USA Today*, November 1990.

James David Barber, "How to Choose a President," *Psychology Today*, May/June 1992.

Michael Barone, "The New Face of American Politics," *National Review*, April 27, 1992.

Alan Brinkley, "America Goes to the Polls," *Business Week*, March 16, 1992.

Michael Duffy, "Wake-Up Call," *Time*, November 18, 1991.

Howard Fineman, "Nasty as They Wanna Be," *Newsweek*, March 9, 1992.

—————————, "Throwing a Mighty Tantrum: The Lure of Third Party Candidates," *Newsweek*, April 27, 1992.

David R. Gergen, "Let's Stop Kidding Ourselves," *U.S. News & World Report*, March 30, 1992.

Marci McDonald, "Campaign Carnival," *Maclean's*, April 13, 1992.

Lance Morrow, "Voters Are Mad as Hell," *Time*, March 2, 1992.

The New York Times, "The Myth of the Black Vote," April 9, 1992.

Newsweek, "Did the Pilgrims Have a PAC?" November 26, 1990.

Janet Novack, "Influence for Sale," *Forbes*, February 20, 1989.

Fiona Smith, "Super PACmen," *Mother Jones*, September/October 1990.

Time, "A Little Help for Some Friends," November 5, 1990.

Michael Waldman, "Quid Pro Whoa: What Your Congressman Shouldn't Do for You," *The New Republic*, March 19, 1990.

Kenneth T. Walsh, "Time for a Makeover," *U.S. News & World Report*, April 20, 1992.

Judy Woodruff, "Can Democracy Survive the Media in the 1990s?" *USA Today*, May 1990.

WORKS CONSULTED

The following books and periodicals were used in the compilation of this book.

R.W. Apple Jr., "How the Campaign Financing System Might Aid Perot," *The New York Times*, April 24, 1992. Author provides statistics on cost of running a presidential campaign. Concludes that Perot would have had to spend $100 million to remain competitive.

John Chancellor, "To Heck with The Primaries," *San Francisco Chronicle*, January 26, 1992. Author believes presidential primaries are inefficient, expensive, drawn-out, and detrimental to the election process. He advocates allowing politicians to choose America's leaders.

Barbara Hinckley, *American Politics and Government*. Glenview, IL: Scott, Foresman and Co., 1990. A textbook on American politics with chapters on elections, campaign finance, and voting.

Carolyn Lockhead, "PAC Donations Jump 14% to $73 Million," *San Francisco Chronicle*, June 9, 1992. Federal Election Commission reports that political action committee contributions rose to $73 million during 1992 campaign season. Provides list of large corporate and PAC donors.

Tom Morganthau, "Checkbook Politics," *Newsweek*, April 2, 1990. Article details economic influence of political action committees (PACs). Encourages campaign finance reform.

A. James Reichly, ed., *Elections American Style*. Washington, DC: Brookings Institution, 1987. A collection of essays and articles focusing on the unique nature of America's elections. Includes chapter on the impact of media on election results.

ORGANIZATIONS TO CONTACT

American Civil Liberties Union (ACLU)
132 W. 43rd St.
New York, NY 10036
(212) 944-9800

The ACLU champions the rights set forth in the Declaration of Independence and the Constitution. Their chapters offer legal support for plaintiffs in voting discrimination cases.

American Enterprise Institute for Public Policy Research (AEI)
1150 17th St. NW
Washington, DC 20036
(202) 862-5800

AEI has published numerous books and pamphlets on topics such as presidential primaries, campaign finance, and the electoral college. After every national election, the institute publishes studies on the results.

Cato Institute
225 Second St. SE
Washington, DC 20003
(202) 546-0200

In accord with the Cato Institute's belief that government should be limited and individual liberty respected, it opposes federal regulation of election campaigns. It has published a number of books and position papers on America's elections.

Churches' Committee for Voter Registration/Education
110 Maryland Ave. NE
Washington, DC 20002
(202) 543-2800

The Churches' Committee is an ecumenical voter participation project formed in 1983. It works to increase the participation of the poor and minorities in the electoral process.

Common Cause
2030 M St. NW
Washington, DC 20036
(202) 833-1200

Common Cause is a nonprofit public interest organization that seeks to reform government ethics, campaign financing, and political action committees.

Democratic Party
Democratic National Committee
430 S. Capitol St. SE
Washington, DC 20003
(202) 863-8000

The Democratic party was founded in 1798 by Thomas Jefferson as the "party of the common man." Among its many stands on the issues, the party calls for more cooperation between government and industry to improve economic growth and for more government support of education and child care.

League of Women Voters
1730 M St. NW
Washington, DC 20036
(202) 429-1965

The league is a voluntary organization of women and men who promote political responsibility through informed and active citizen participation in government. The league has sponsored debates between presidential candidates at both the primary and national levels.

Republican Party
Republican National Committee
310 First St. SE
Washington, DC 20001
(202) 662-1355

The Republican party was founded in 1856. Four years later, it elected its first president, Abraham Lincoln. Among its many stands on the issues, the party advocates less government regulation of the economy, lower taxes, and a continued strengthening of American military forces.

INDEX

WITHDRAWN

No longer the property of the
Boston Public Library.
Sale of this material benefits the Library.